Wonderful ways to prepare

HORS D'OEUV
FIRST COURSES

by JO ANN SHIRLEY

OTHER TITLES IN THIS SERIES

Printed in Canada/Cover Printed in USA

Wonderful ways to prepare

HORS D'OEUVRES & FIRST COURSES

PLAYMORE INC NEW YORK USA
UNDER ARRANGEMENT WITH
I. WALDMAN & SON INC

AYERS & JAMES PTY LTD
CROWS NEST AUSTRALIA

STAFFORD PEMBERTON PUBLISHING
KNUTSFORD UNITED KINGDOM

FIRST PUBLISHED 1978

PUBLISHED IN THE USA
BY PLAYMORE INC.
UNDER ARRANGEMENT WITH I. WALDMAN & SON INC.

PUBLISHED IN AUSTRALIA
BY AYERS & JAMES PTY. LTD.
CROWS NEST.   AUSTRALIA

PUBLISHED IN THE UNITED KINGDOM
BY STAFFORD PEMBERTON PUBLISHING
KNUTSFORD CHESIRE

ISBN 0 86908 054 7

Contents

Hors d'œuvres

Dip for Raw Vegetables

1 cup (250 g) sour cream
1 tablespoon chopped
   fresh basil
1 teaspoon paprika
chili powder to taste
salt

Mix all ingredients and chill well. Serve with fresh crispy raw vegetables such as carrot sticks, green and red pepper slices, cauliflower flowerets, celery stalks, radish roses, cherry tomatoes and zucchini.

Ham and Cheese Bites

6 slices white bread,
   crust removed
½ lb (250 g) Mozzarella cheese
3 slices ham
butter or margarine

1. Butter the bread.
2. Place a slice of Mozzarella cheese and a slice of ham on three pieces of bread. Cover with the other three pieces. Press together firmly.
3. Fry gently in butter or margarine until golden brown on both sides.
4. Cut each sandwich into quarters. Serve hot.

Chicken and Clam Spread

½ lb (250 g) minced clams
1 cup minced chicken
¼ lb (125 g) cream cheese
1 tablespoon finely
   chopped onion

1 tablespoon mayonnaise
salt and pepper
toast rounds
parsley

1. Drain clams, reserving liquid. Mix with chicken and cream cheese.
2. Add enough clam liquid to make clam mixture smooth.
3. Add onion, mayonnaise and seasonings to taste.
4. Serve on toast rounds and sprinkle with parsley.

Olives in Cheese

¼ lb (125 g) cream cheese
1 teaspoon Worcestershire sauce
cream
20 large stuffed olives
¼ lb (125 g) salted almonds,
   chopped

1. Mix the cheese with the Worcestershire sauce. Add enough cream to make a thick, smooth paste.
2. Roll olives in the mixture. Be sure that each is well coated.
3. Roll in the chopped almonds.

Dip for Shrimp

1 cup (250 ml) mayonnaise
curry powder and chilli
   powder to taste
1 clove garlic, crushed
¼ cup (62.5 ml) chili sauce

Combine all ingredients and chill well. Serve with cold cooked shrimp or deep fried shrimp.

French Cheese Sandwiches

16 slices bread
1 lb (500 g) Swiss
  or Gruyere cheese

butter or margarine
1 cup (250 ml) milk
3 eggs

1. Remove crusts from bread, butter it and make a sandwich with the cheese. Press down firmly so the sandwich sticks together.
2. Mix the milk and eggs together, beating well.
3. Dip the sandwiches in the egg and milk mixture.
4. Fry in hot butter or margarine until very brown on both sides. Cook slowly so cheese has time to melt.
5. Cut each sandwich into four triangles and serve immediately.

Stuffed Eggs with Caviar

1 dozen eggs,
  hard-boiled
1 teaspoon dry mustard
4 tablespoons mayonnaise

3 teaspoons finely chopped
  chives
salt and pepper
caviar

1. Cut eggs in half lengthwise and remove egg yolks.
2. Mash egg yolks with mustard, mayonnaise and chives.
3. Season to taste with salt and pepper.
4. Fill egg whites with the mixture and sprinkle each egg with caviar.

Lobster Croutes

4 oz (125 g) lobster (or crabmeat)	salt and pepper
2 shallots, chopped	1 tablespoon cream
1 tablespoon (20 g) butter or margarine	1 tomato
curry powder to taste	6 rounds of buttered toast
	chopped parsley

1. Chop the lobster or crabmeat into small bits.
2. Melt the butter or margarine in a saucepan and saute the shallots with the curry powder and salt and pepper to taste.
3. Add the lobster or crabmeat and cook for one minute.
4. Stir in the cream.
5. Place a slice of tomato on each round of toast, pile the lobster mixture on top and heat thoroughly in a hot oven.
6. Sprinkle with chopped parsley before serving.

Curried Fish Balls

¼ lb (125 g) cold cooked fish	lemon juice
2 tablespoons mashed potato	½ tablespoon (10 g) butter or margarine
salt and pepper	egg and bread crumbs to coat
curry powder to taste	oil to deep fry
½ tablespoon beaten egg	

1. Mix together the fish, potato, salt, pepper, curry powder, beaten egg, lemon juice and butter or margarine in a saucepan. Cook over a low heat for two minutes. Cool.
2. Shape into small balls. Coat with egg and bread crumbs. Chill for ½ hour.
3. Fry in deep oil until golden brown.

Potato Cubes

6 medium potatoes
¼ cup (62.5 g) sour cream
½ cup (125 ml) mayonnaise
curry powder to taste
salt and pepper

1. Peel the potatoes and cook in salted boiling water until tender but still firm.
2. When cool, cut the potatoes in small cubes.
3. Mix the sour cream and the mayonnaise.
4. Season to taste with the curry powder, salt and pepper.
5. Combine the potatoes and the mayonnaise mixture. Toss lightly but thoroughly.
6. Sprinkle with chopped parsley if desired.
7. Serve with toothpicks.

Blue Cheese Spread

½ lb (250 g) blue cheese
1 teaspoon Worcestershire
sauce
mayonnaise
rounds of toast

1. Press cheese through a sieve.
2. Add Worcestershire and mix well.
3. Add enough mayonnaise to hold the mixture together.
4. Serve on rounds of toast.

11

Salmon-Stuffed Eggs

12 hard-boiled eggs
small can salmon
½ cup (125 g) butter
    or margarine
1 teaspoon Worcestershire sauce
salt and pepper

1. Shell eggs and cut in half lengthwise. Remove yolks.
2. Sieve egg yolks and salmon or purée in an electric blender.
3. Soften the butter or margarine.
4. Add butter to the salmon mixture and mix well.
5. Add the Worcestershire sauce and season to taste with salt and pepper. Mix thoroughly.
6. Stuff the egg whites with the mixture.

Bacon and Cheese Rolls

½ lb (250 g) bacon
20 slices thinly sliced
    bread (very fresh)
butter or margarine

½ cup (60 g) Parmesan cheese
4 tablespoons minced parsley
paprika

1. Cook bacon until very crisp. Drain and crumble into small bits.
2. Cut crusts from bread and butter it.
3. Sprinkle the bacon down the middle of the bread.
4. Put Parmesan cheese and parsley on top of the bacon.
5. Sprinkle paprika on top.
6. Roll each slice up tightly and secure with a toothpick.
7. Broil until lightly browned.

Curried Beef Puffs

2 cloves garlic, crushed
½ onion, chopped
curry powder to taste
2 tablespoons (40 g) butter
  or margarine

½ lb (250 g) ground beef
1 tablespoon lemon juice
½ teaspoon salt
pastry

1. Sauté the garlic, onion and curry powder in the butter for five minutes.
2. Add meat and cook until meat is thoroughly browned.
3. Add lemon juice and salt and mix well.
4. Roll out pastry and cut into 2 in (5 cm) rounds.
5. Place a little meat mixture on one round, cover with another and pinch edges together.
6. Bake in a very hot oven, 450°F (230°C) gas or 475°F (250°C) electric for 15 minutes or until brown.

Eggplant Spread

1 medium eggplant
1 large onion
1 clove garlic
3 medium tomatoes

½ cup (125 ml) olive oil
1 teaspoon salt
1 tablespoon finely minced
  parsley

1. Cook eggplant in a moderate oven 375°F (190°C) for ½ hour to 45 minutes.
2. Allow to cool slightly. Peel carefully and dice.
3. Peel onion, garlic and tomatoes and chop finely.
4. Mix the eggplant with the onion, garlic and tomatoes.
5. Add olive oil, salt and parsley and mix thoroughly.
6. Chill well before serving with toast fingers.

Crabmeat and Cheese Balls

2 tablespoons (40 g) butter
  or margarine
½ small onion, minced
2 tablespoons flour
½ cup chicken stock
1 cup crabmeat

pinch cayenne
salt and pepper
1 tablespoon cream
3 tablespoons each grated Parmesan
  or Swiss cheese
toast (crusts removed)

1. Sauté onion in 1 tablespoon butter or margarine until transparent.
2. Add one tablespoon flour and mix well.
3. Gradually add the stock, stirring constantly.
4. Add crabmeat. Season to taste with cayenne, salt and pepper. Set mixture aside.
5. Melt remaining tablespoon of butter and stir in remaining tablespoon of flour.
6. Add cream and cheese and cook, stirring constantly until cheeses are melted.
7. When cheese mixture is cool, form into little balls.
8. Spread crab mixture on toast, top with cheese ball and cook in very hot oven 450°F (230°C) for five minutes.

Savory Rounds

3 hard-boiled eggs
2 tablespoons finely chopped
  red pepper
½ teaspoon dry mustard
1 tablespoon grated Parmesan
  cheese

¼ teaspoon salt
1 tablespoon minced parsley
¼ cup (62.5 g) butter
  or margarine
tomato sauce
toast rounds

1. Chop eggs finely and mix with pepper, mustard, cheese, salt, parsley and butter.
2. Add enough tomato sauce to moisten.
3. Spread on toast rounds and cook in very hot oven 450°F (230°C) for five minutes.

Crabmeat and Cucumber Rounds

2 cups crabmeat
¼ cup (62.5 ml) mayonnaise
½ teaspoon Worcestershire sauce
1 large cucumber

salt and pepper
sauteed toast rounds
chopped parsley

1. Shred crabmeat and mix it with the mayonnaise. (Add more mayonnaise if necessary to bind.)
2. Add Worcestershire sauce and mix well.
3. Peel cucumber and chop finely. Season with salt and pepper.
4. Spread a little cucumber on each toast round. Cover with crabmeat mixture.
5. Broil until lightly browned.

Ham Dip

½ lb (250 g) cooked ham
¼ cup mayonnaise
2 tablespoons chili sauce
1 tablespoon prepared mustard
½ teaspoon brown sugar

1. Mince or grind the ham.
2. Mix the ham with the mayonnaise, chili sauce, mustard and sugar.
3. If necessary, add more mayonnaise to obtain a better consistency.

Guacamole

1 large avocado
1 tablespoon lemon juice
chili powder to taste

1 clove garlic, crushed
2 tablespoons mayonnaise
salt

1. Peel avocado, remove seed and mash avocado.
2. Add lemon juice and mix well.
3. Add chili powder, garlic and mayonnaise.
4. Season to taste with salt.

Serve with corn chips.

Garlic and Walnut Spread

1 cup (120 g) walnuts
3 cloves garlic, crushed
4 slices bread, crust removed
3 tablespoons vinegar

2 teaspoons olive oil
1 teaspoon minced parsley
salt

1. Crush walnuts or whirl in an electric blender.
2. Add garlic and mix well.
3. Soak the bread in water. Squeeze out and break the bread up.
4. Mix the bread with the nuts and garlic until it has formed a paste.
5. Slowly add vinegar and oil. Add the parsley and mix well.
6. Season to taste with salt. Serve with toast.

Chicken Liver Pate

1 cup (250 g) butter
1 lb (500 g) chicken livers
¼ cup brandy

3 scallions, chopped
½ teaspoon salt
freshly ground black pepper

1. Saute the chicken livers in the butter until cooked.
2. Purée in an electric blender with the brandy, scallions, salt and pepper.
3. Put pate into a dish and refrigerate for 24 hours before serving.
4. Serve with hot toast.

Tomatoes on Toast

6 small tomatoes
bread cut into rounds
    (to fit tomatoes)
butter or margarine
mustard
mayonnaise

1. Slice tomatoes to desired thickness.
2. Saute breads rounds in butter or margarine until golden brown.
3. Put a tomato slice on each round and spread a little mustard on top.
4. Spread mayonnaise fairly thickly over the mustard.
5. Cook in broiler for three to five minutes or until the mayonnaise puffs up.

Tomato Caviar Rounds

1 lb (500 g) tomatoes
¼ lb (125 g) cream cheese
1 tablespoon cream
1 tablespoon minced onion

¼ cup mayonnaise
1 small jar caviar
rounds of toast

1. Peel the tomatoes and remove the seeds. Chop finely.
2. Combine the cream cheese, cream and onion. Mix thoroughly.
3. Spread cream cheese mixture on the toast, top with chopped tomato and a little mayonnaise. Sprinkle caviar on top.

Cream Cheese Balls

½ lb (250 g) cream cheese
1 tablespoon chopped onion
1 tablespoon chopped chives
2 carrots, grated

1. Cream together cream cheese, onion and chives.
2. Form into small balls.
3. Roll in grated carrots and serve with toothpicks.

Variations:
Mix parsley with the cream cheese and roll in finely chopped green and red pepper.
Mix chives with the cream cheese and roll in chopped nuts.

Bacon Rolls

1 lb (500 g) bacon
prepared mustard
prepared horseradish sauce

1. Cut bacon in half.
2. Spread mustard and horseradish on bacon.
3. Roll up and secure with a toothpick.
4. Broil until bacon is cooked.

Stuffed Prunes

1 lb (500 g) prunes
¼ lb (125 g) cream cheese
½ cup chopped walnuts

1. Remove seeds from prunes. Keep prunes whole.
2. Combine cream cheese and walnuts. Mix thoroughly.
3. Stuff cream cheese mixture into prunes.

(Variation: Mix cream cheese with pineapple bits.)

Ham Rolls

¼ lb (125 g) cream cheese
8 stuffed green olives
2 teaspoons prepared
**   horseradish sauce**
2 tablespoons cream
salt and pepper
ham slices

1. Combine cream cheese with chopped olives, horseradish sauce, cream.
2. Season to taste with salt and pepper.
3. Spread on ham slices. Roll up and secure with a toothpick.

Crabmeat and Bacon Rolls

½ cup (125 ml) tomato
**   juice**
1 egg, beaten
1 cup (125 g) dry
**   bread crumbs**

1 teaspoon chopped parsley
1 can crabmeat
12 slices bacon, cut in half

1. Mix tomato juice and egg.
2. Add bread crumbs, parsley and crab meat.
3. Season to taste with salt and pepper.
4. Spread mixture onto bacon slices, roll up and fasten with a toothpick.
5. Cook in broiler, turning often, until bacon is evenly browned.

Avocado Fingers

1 large avocado
¼ teaspoon salt
¼ teaspoon paprika

2 teaspoons lemon juice
bacon
toast strips

1. Peel the avocado and remove the seed.
2. Mash the avocado and combine with salt, paprika and lemon juice.
3. Spread the mixture on toast strips and top with bacon.
4. Put in broiler and cook until bacon crisps.

Parsley Wheels

toast rounds
butter
chopped parsley
1 cup chopped cooked chicken

3 tablespoons mayonnaise
2 tablespoons minced onion
salt and pepper

1. Spread edges of toast rounds with softened butter. Roll the edges in chopped parsley. Set aside.
2. Combine chicken, mayonnaise, onion and salt and pepper.
3. Spread on toast.

Anchovy Puffs

½ cup (¼ lb) butter or margarine
¼ lb (125 g) cream cheese
1 cup flour
anchovy paste

1. Blend butter with cream cheese. Mix with the flour.
2. Roll very thinly and cut into 2 inch (5 cm) rounds.
3. Spread with anchovy paste and fold in half.
4. Bake in hot oven, 400°F (200°C) for ten minutes, or until brown.

Anchovies and Eggs

1 small onion, sliced	2 cups (500 ml) milk
2 tablespoons (40 g) butter	2 tablespoons chopped parsley
1 can anchovy fillets	freshly ground black pepper
5 eggs	

1. Sauté the onion in the butter until it is transparent.
2. Line a greased baking dish with the anchovy fillets.
3. Beat the eggs with the milk.
4. Add the parsley and mix well.
5. Pour the egg mixture into the baking dish on top of the anchovies.
6. Sprinkle with pepper.
7. Bake in a moderately hot oven 375°F (190°C) for 30 minutes or until eggs are set.
8. Cut into small pieces and serve on toast.

Cheese Straws

⅔ cup flour	½ cup grated cheese
salt and cayenne pepper	1 egg yolk
pinch dry mustard	a little water
2 tablespoons (40 g) butter or margarine	

1. Mix together flour, salt, cayenne and mustard.
2. Add the butter and mix well.
3. Add the cheese and blend thoroughly.
4. Pour in the egg yolk and enough water to make a stiff dough.
5. Roll the dough out thinly and cut into narrow straws.
6. Bake in a moderately hot oven 375°F (190°C) for five to seven minutes or until golden brown.

Sour Cream and Chili Dip

1 cup (125 ml) sour cream
1 tablespoon chili sauce
1 teaspoon dry mustard
1 medium onion, grated
1 teaspoon Worcestershire sauce

1 tablespoon chopped chives
1 tablespoon chopped parsley
½ teaspoon salt
¼ teaspoon pepper

1. Mix all ingredients thoroughly.
2. Chill for several hours before serving.

Sour Cream and Cottage Cheese Dip

½ cup (125 g) sour cream
½ cup (125 g) cottage cheese
2 tablespoons mayonnaise
1 tablespoon chili sauce
1 tablespoon chopped chives

1 tablespoon chopped parsley
1 tablespoon minced
  green pepper
salt and pepper

1. Mix together all ingredients.
2. Season to taste with salt and pepper.
3. Chill for several hours.

Anchovy and Sour Cream Dip

3 anchovies
1 cup (250 g) sour cream
1 tablespoon chopped chives
1 tablespoon chopped parsley
1 tablespoon lemon juice

1. Mash anchovies.
2. Add the anchovies to the sour cream, chives, parsley and lemon juice and mix thoroughly.

21

Hot Meat Balls

1 lb (500 g) finely ground beef
1½ teaspoons salt
2 teaspoons dry mustard
1 clove garlic, crushed

1 onion, grated
1 teaspoon Worcestershire sauce
4 tablespoons minced parsley

1. Mix together all the ingredients.
2. Form into small balls.
3. Cook in hot oil until brown on outside but still pink on the inside.
4. Serve with toothpicks.

Celery and Caviar

celery stalks
½ cup sour cream
small jar red caviar
1 teaspoon lemon juice

1. Cut celery stalks into 2 in (5 cm) pieces.
2. Combine the sour cream, caviar and lemon juice.
3. Fill celery pieces with the caviar mixture.

Celery and Blue Cheese

celery stalks
¼ lb (125 g) blue cheese
½ cup sour cream
1 onion, grated

1 teaspoon freshly ground
  black pepper
chopped chives

1. Cut celery stalks into 2 in (5 cm) pieces.
2. Mix together blue cheese, sour cream, onion and black pepper.
3. Fill celery pieces with the blue cheese mixture and sprinkle with chopped chives.

Marinated Mushrooms

1 lb (500 g) button mushrooms
1 cup (250 ml) olive oil
⅓ cup (83 ml) vinegar
2 cloves garlic, crushed

1 teaspoon dry mustard
1 teaspoon salt
½ teaspoon pepper

1. To clean mushrooms wipe with a damp cloth.
2. Combine oil, vinegar, garlic, mustard, salt and pepper. Mix well.
3. Marinate the mushrooms in the dressing for several hours.
4. Drain and serve with toothpicks.

Chicken Liver Rolls

½ lb (250 g) chicken livers
butter or margarine
bacon

1. Sauté the chicken livers in the butter or margarine until cooked.
2. Remove from the pan and cut into bite-size pieces.
3. Wrap each piece in bacon, secure with a toothpick and cook in griller until bacon is crisp.

Fried Scallops

½ lb (250 g) scallops
flour
1 egg, beaten
bread crumbs

1. Pour boiling water over scallops, let stand for one minute, drain and dry.
2. Season with salt and pepper, roll in flour, dip in egg, roll in bread crumbs and fry in deep fat.
3. Drain and serve with toothpicks around a bowl of tartare sauce.

Smoked Salmon Rolls

¼ lb (125 g) smoked salmon
3 tablespoons cream cheese
1 tablespoon horseradish sauce

1. Mix cream cheese and horseradish sauce together.
2. Spread smoked salmon with the mixture and roll up. Secure with a toothpick.

Lettuce Rolls

¼ lb (125 g) blue cheese
2 tablespoons anchovy paste
pinch of cayenne
lettuce

1. Mix together the blue cheese, anchovy paste and cayenne. Chill.
2. Place a small amount on a piece of lettuce and roll up. Secure with a toothpick.

Anchovy Canapes

rounds of rye bread
anchovy paste
anchovy fillets
minced raw mushrooms
butter or margarine

1. Spread rounds of rye bread with anchovy paste mixed with a little butter. or margarine.
2. Place anchovy fillet on top and cover with minced mushrooms.
3. Sprinkle with paprika, dot with butter and bake in a moderate oven 350°F (180°C) for ten minutes.

Stuffed Mushrooms

1 lb (500 g) large mushrooms
¼ lb (125 g) ham
white sauce
chopped chives

1. Remove stems from mushrooms.
2. Finely chop ham and mushroom stems. Add a little white sauce to make a paste. Season to taste with salt and pepper.
3. Fill mushrooms with the ham mixture and bake until brown in a moderate oven 350°F (180°C).

Mushroom and Clam Canapes

¼ lb (125 g) mushrooms
1 tablespoon minced onion
3 tablespoons (60 g) butter
   or margarine
2 tablespoons flour
⅔ cup (166 ml) cream

1 can clams, minced
2 tablespoons grated cheese
2 egg yolks, well beaten
salt and cayenne
2 teaspoons lemon juice
toast

1. Sauté the mushrooms and onion in the butter or margarine.
2. Add the flour and cream and cook until the mixture thickens.
3. Add the clams and one tablespoon of cheese and mix well.
4. Add the egg yolks and lemon juice and season to taste with salt and cayenne.
5. Spread on toast, sprinkle with remaining cheese and bake in a moderate oven 350°F (180°C) for five minutes.

Anchovies in Pastry

1 cup grated cheddar
   cheese
½ cup (125 g) butter
   or margarine

1 cup flour
¼ teaspoon salt
milk
anchovy fillets

1. Mix the cheese with butter or margarine, flour and salt.
2. Add enough milk to form a stiff dough.
3. Roll very thinly and cut into strips twice as large as the anchovy fillet.
4. Lay anchovy fillet on strip and fold over like an envelope. Pinch edges of dough together.
5. Bake in a moderate oven 350°F (180°F) until brown.

Nut Cheese Balls

¼ lb (125 g) blue cheese
¼ lb (125 g) cream cheese
2 tablespoons (40 g) butter
   or margarine

1 teaspoon Worcestershire sauce
1 teaspoon paprika
pinch cayenne
½ cup ground walnuts

1. Mix together the blue cheese, cream cheese, butter or margarine, Worcestershire sauce, paprika and cayenne.
2. Form into small balls.
3. Roll in ground walnuts and chill.

First Courses

Quiche Lorraine

½ lb (250 g) bacon, lean
¼ lb (125 g) Swiss cheese
¼ lb (125 g) cheddar cheese
4 eggs
2 cups (500 ml) cream
1 teaspoon salt
pinch of sugar
pinch of nutmeg
cayenne
black pepper
large unbaked pie shell

1. Cook bacon until crisp and break into small pieces.
2. Beat eggs, cream and seasonings just long enough to thoroughly mix.
3. Rub a little butter or margarine on the surface of the pie shell. Sprinkle the bacon over the bottom.
4. Grate the cheese and put over the bacon.
5. Pour the egg mixture over the cheese.
6. Bake in a 450°F (230°C) oven for ten minutes. Reduce heat to 300°F (150°C) and bake until the eggs have set (25-30 minutes).

Serves 6-8.

Avocado Mousse

½ cup (125 ml) cold water
1 tablespoon gelatin
1 large avocado, mashed
½ teaspoon salt
2 teaspoons Worcestershire sauce

1 cup (250 ml) cream
½ cup (125 ml) mayonnaise
lettuce leaves
lemon, sliced

1. Dissolve gelatin in cold water in a saucepan. Stir over a very low heat until gelatin completely dissolves. Set aside.
2. Mix together the avocado, salt and Worcestershire sauce.
3. Mix together the cream and the mayonnaise. Add to the avocado mixture. Mix well.
4. Mix in the gelatin. Stir well.
5. Pour mixture into an oiled mold. Chill until firm.
6. Unmold onto a bed of lettuce.

Serves 4-6.

Ham Mousse

¾ cup (186 ml) water
1 tablespoon gelatin
2 cups ham, chopped
1 teaspoon prepared mustard

pinch of cayenne
1 cup (250 ml) cream, whipped
1 tablespoon chopped parsley

1. Dissolve gelatin in cold water in a saucepan. Stir over a very low heat until gelatin completely dissolves. Set aside.
2. Mix the ham with the mustard and cayenne.
3. Stir in the dissolved gelatin.
4. Fold in the whipped cream.
5. Pour mixture into an oiled mold. Chill until firm.
6. Unmold and garnish with chopped parsley.

Serves 4.

Tarte Nicoise

Pastry:
1 cup flour
2½ tablespoons (50 g) butter
    or margarine
1 egg yolk
2-3 tablespoons cold water
½ teaspoon salt

1. Sift flour into a mixing bowl. Add butter or margarine and mix well.
2. Mix together cold water, egg yolk and salt. Add to flour and butter mixture and mix until it form a dough ball.
3. Roll out and line an 8-inch (20 cm) flan or pie tin. Bake in a 350°F (180°C) oven for 15 minutes.

Filling:

4 medium tomatoes,
    seeded and chopped
½ cup grated cheese
¼ cup dried bread crumbs
2 tablespoons chopped
    parsley

1 tablespoon chopped chives
8 black olives, seeded
    and quartered
salt and pepper

1. Mix all ingredients together and season to taste with salt and pepper.
2. Spoon onto cooked pastry shell.

Custard:
2 eggs
½ cup (125 ml) cream
salt and pepper

1. Beat eggs and combine with cream. Add a little salt and pepper.
2. Pour over the tomato mixture and cook in a 350°F (180°C) oven for ½ hour or until the tart is set.

Serves 4-6.

Tomato Aspic with Green Beans

2　packets lemon gelatin
2　cups tomato juice (500 ml)
1½　cups (375 ml) tomato soup
　　(undiluted)
2　tablespoons lemon juice

1. Dissolve the gelatin in the boiling tomato juice. Cool slightly and add the tomato soup and lemon juice.
2. Pour into a large oiled ring mold. Chill until firm.
3. Unmold and fill center with green beans and Vinaigrette Dressing.

Cook 1 lb (500 g) fresh green beans in boiling salted water for 5-7 minutes. Drain and marinate in Vinaigrette Dressing for several hours. Drain off excess dressing before serving.

Vinaigrette Dressing:	
3　tablespoons sweet pickle relish	½　cup (125 ml) salad oil
	1　teaspoon salt
3　tablespoons chopped parsley	½　teaspoon sugar
	6　tablespoons vinegar

Blend all ingredients and pour over green beans.

Serves 6-8.

Fish Sticks Curry

1 lb (500 g) fish sticks
1 cup (250 ml) water
1½ cups (375 ml) cream
3 onions, chopped
1 teaspoon salt

½ teaspoon pepper
curry powder to taste
3 tablespoons chopped
parsley

1. Place fish sticks in a buttered baking dish and cook in a 350°F (180°C) oven for ten minutes.
2. Combine water, cream, onions, salt, pepper and curry powder.
3. Pour over the fish sticks and bake for another fifteen minutes.
4. Sprinkle parsley over the top and serve immediately.

Serves 6.

Ham and Chicken Mousse

1 tablespoon gelatin
2 tablespoons cold water
1 teaspoon salt
pinch of cayenne
3 egg yolks, slightly beaten
1 cup (250 ml) hot
chicken stock
1 cup chopped ham

1 cup chopped chicken,
cooked
1 small onion, minced
3 tablespoons oil
2 tablespoons vinegar
½ cup (125 ml) cream,
whipped
lettuce leaves

1. Soak the gelatin in the cold water.
2. In the top of a double boiler, mix salt, cayenne and egg yolks.
3. Stir in the stock and cook over boiling water until thick, stirring constantly.
4. Add gelatin and stir until dissolved. Cool.
5. Fold in ham, chicken, onion, oil, vinegar and cream. Pour into a mold and chill until firm.
6. Unmold onto lettuce leaves.

Serves 4-6.

Stuffed Mushrooms

12 large mushrooms
2 tablespoons olive
   or salad oil
1 small onion, chopped
1 clove garlic, crushed
4 anchovy fillets, chopped
1 tablespoon chopped
   parsley
1 tablespoon chopped chives

½ teaspoon salt
½ teaspoon pepper
1 slice bread, crust removed,
   soaked in water and squeezed dry
1 egg
2 tablespoons bread crumbs
1 tablespoon olive
   or salad oil

1. Remove stems from mushrooms, chop and saute in 2 tablespoons oil with onion and garlic for 5 minutes. Add anchovies, parsley, chives, salt and pepper and cook for a further five minutes.
2. Remove from heat, add bread and egg and mix thoroughly.
3. Fill mushroom caps with stuffing, sprinkle with bread crumbs, then with oil and put in a greased baking dish. Cook in a hot oven 400°F (200°C) for 20 minutes.

Serves 4.

Asparagus with Hollandaise Sauce

2 bunches fresh asparagus
½ cup (125 g) butter
4 egg yolks
2 teaspoons lemon juice
salt and pepper

1. Wash and trim the asparagus. Cook (boil or steam) until tender. Drain.
2. In the top of a double boiler put a quarter of the butter and the 4 egg yolks. Place over hot but not boiling water. Stir constantly with a wooden spoon until butter and eggs are well mixed.
3. Add the remaining butter bit by bit whisking the mixture constantly until the sauce is thick.
4. Remove from heat and beat well for two minutes.
5. Add lemon juice and salt and pepper to taste. Mix well.
6. Place over hot water again and beat for a further 2-3 minutes.
7. If the sauce curdles, add 1-2 tablespoons cold water and mix well.
8. Serve sauce over hot asparagus.

Serves 6.

Onion a la Greque

2 lb (1 kg) small onions,
  peeled
2½ cups (625 ml) water
1¼ cups (300 ml) dry
  white wine
¾ cup sugar
½ cups raisins

4 tablespoons tomato paste
4 tablespoons olive
  or salad oil
3 tablespoons vinegar
salt and pepper
chopped parsley

1. In a large saucepan combine the onions, water, wine, sugar, raisins, tomato paste and oil. Bring to a boil.
2. Add vinegar and salt and pepper to taste.
3. Simmer for about 40 minutes.
4. Chill and serve garnished with parsley.

Serves 6-8.

Zucchini a la Greque

2 small onions
 thinly sliced
3 tablespoons olive oil
1 clove garlic, crushed
½ cup (125 ml) dry white wine

salt and pepper
1½ lb (750 g) zucchini
½ lb (250 g) tomatoes
pinch of oregano

1. Sauté the onions in the oil until transparent.
2. Add the garlic and white wine. Mix in a little salt and pepper.
3. Wipe zucchini with a damp cloth. Cut off a slice at each end and discard. Cut the zucchini into slices.
4. Peel the tomatoes and cut into quarters. Remove seeds.
5. Combine the zucchini and tomatoes in the frypan with the oil and wine and cook gently for ten minutes.
6. Add a little oregano. Season to taste with salt and pepper and cool.

Serves 4-6.

Quick Mushrooms and Shrimp

1 large can button
 mushrooms
2 tablespoons (40 g) butter
 or margarine
½ cup flour
1¼ cups (300 ml) milk

1 cup (250 ml) cream
salt and pepper
½ lb (250 g) canned shrimp
1 tablespoon sherry
chopped parsley
fried bread crumbs

1. Sauté the mushrooms in the butter for two minutes.
2. Add the flour, mix well and cook for another two minutes.
3. Slowly add the milk and cream. Stirring constantly, cook until sauce is thick and smooth.
4. Season to taste with salt and pepper.
5. Drain the shrimp and add to the sauce with the sherry. Reheat.
6. Serve in individual dishes and sprinkle with parsley and fried bread crumbs.

Serves 4.

Stuffed Red Peppers

6 large red peppers
¾ cup (186 ml) olive
  or salad oil
1½ cups dry bread crumbs
4 tablespoons raisins
15 black olives,
  pitted and chopped
8 anchovy fillets, chopped
1 teaspoon dry basil

1 tablespoon chopped parsley
2 tablespoons capers
1 tablespoon chopped chives
1 teaspoon salt
½ teaspoon pepper
6 tablespoons olive
  or salad oil
¾ cup (186 ml) tomato
  sauce

1. Wash peppers. Cut off top and remove the seeds.
2. Mix together oil, bread crumbs, raisins, olives, anchovies, basil, parsley, capers, chives, salt and pepper. Mix very well.
3. Fill peppers and place them in a deep baking dish. Pour the 6 tablespoons of oil over the peppers and top each with the tomato sauce.
4. Bake in a 375°F (190°C) oven for one hour.

Serves 6.

Blue Cheese Mold

½ lb (250 g) blue cheese
½ lb (250 g) cream cheese
1 cup finely chopped
  celery leaves
½ green pepper, chopped
1 tablespoon minced onion
1 tablespoon (20 g)
  melted butter

1 tablespoon Worcestershire
  sauce
salt and pepper
½ lb (250 g) walnuts, chopped
2 tablespoons chopped parsley

1. Mix together all ingredients except the nuts and parsley. Form into a ball.
2. Mix the walnuts with the parsley.
3. Roll the cheese ball in the nuts and parsley. Chill.
4. Serve with hot toast.

Serves 6-8.

Tomato Pie

2 cans tomatoes (2 lbs, 3 oz)
4 tablespoons chopped parsley
2 tablespoons chopped chives
salt and pepper
butter
3 cups fresh bread crumbs

1. Drain tomatoes and chop coarsely.
2. Butter a pie dish and line with bread crumbs. Press the bread crumbs down firmly.
3. Place tomatoes on top of breadcrumbs and sprinkle with parsley, chives, salt and pepper. Dot with butter.
4. Cover with more bread crumbs, dot with more butter and cook in a moderate oven 350°F (180°C) for ½ hour to 40 minutes.

Serves 6.

Spinach and Red Pepper Tart

1 lb (500 g) spinach
1 red pepper
1 cup (250 ml) tomato puree
¼ cup (62.5 ml) tomato paste
2 cloves garlic
olive or salad oil
salt and pepper
5 oz (155 g) shortcrust pastry

1. Roll out the pastry, line a pie tin and bake in a hot oven 400°F (200°C) for five minutes.
2. Wash, cook and drain the spinach. Heat a little oil in a saucepan, add the spinach, garlic, salt and pepper and cook for about ten minutes.
3. Remove the seeds from the pepper and cook in salted boiling water for ten minutes. Drain and chop.
4. Mix together the tomato purée and tomato paste and heat. Pour into the pie tin. Put the spinach on top of the tomato sauce and sprinkle with the chopped pepper.
5. Bake in a 375°F (190°C) oven for about twenty minutes.

Serves 4-6.

Baked Asparagus

1 lb (500 g) fresh
asparagus
3 tablespoons (60 g) butter
or margarine
½ onion, chopped
1 celery stalk celery, chopped
2 tablespoons minced parsley
1 tablespoon chopped chives
2 tablespoons grated
Parmesan cheese

2 tablespoons fresh
bread crumbs
4 tomatoes, peeled,
seeded and diced
salt and pepper
pinch of oregano
pinch of thyme

1. Wash asparagus well.
2. Melt butter or margarine in a baking dish. Line the bottom with the asparagus spears.
3. Sprinkle onion, celery, parsley, chives, cheese, bread crumbs, tomatoes, salt and pepper, oregano and thyme on top. Cover and bake for 45 mins. in a 375°F (190°C) oven.

Serves 4.

Avocado Eggs

12 eggs, hard-boiled
1 avocado
1 small clove garlic,
crushed
1 teaspoon salt

¼ teaspoon black pepper
1 teaspoon dry mustard
4 tablespoons mayonnaise
bunch of watercress

1. Mash the avocado and mix well with garlic, pepper, salt, mustard and mayonnaise.
2. Cut eggs in half lengthwise and remove egg yolks. Mash egg yolks well and add to the avocado mixture. Mix well.
3. Fill egg whites with the avocado and egg yolk mixture and serve on individual dishes with watercress.

Serves 6.

Caviar Mold

1 tablespoon gelatin
½ cup (125 ml) milk
1 cup (250 ml) mayonnaise
1 tablespoon lemon juice
1 cup (250 ml) cream, whipped
¼ lb (125 g) black caviar

1. Dissolve the gelatin in cold milk. Heat in the top of a double boiler until completely dissolved. Cool.
2. Add mayonnaise, lemon juice and whipped cream. Stir in the caviar.
3. Pour mixture into an oiled mold and chill until firm.
4. Unmold onto a bed of lettuce.

Serves 6-8.

Barley-Mushroom Mold

1½ cups (315 g) barley
4½ cups (1¼ liters) water
1 teaspoon caraway seed
1 teaspoon salt
3 tablespoons (60 g) butter
  or margarine
½ lb (250 g) mushrooms,
  sliced

2 tablespoons chopped parsley
1 clove garlic, crushed
1 teaspoon salt
¼ teaspoon pepper
¼ teaspoon marjoram
¼ cup (62.5 g) butter
  or margarine
¼ cup (62.5 ml) water

1. Put barley, water, caraway seeds and salt in a saucepan, cover and simmer for one hour or until tender.
2. Melt the three tablespoons butter in a saucepan and sauté the mushrooms, parsley, garlic, salt, pepper and marjoram for five minutes. Add the ¼ cup butter and ¼ cup water and heat.
3. Drain barley and add to the mushroom mixture.
4. Pour into a well oiled ring mold, place in a pan of water and bake for 45 minutes in a 350°F (180°C) oven.

Serves 6-8.

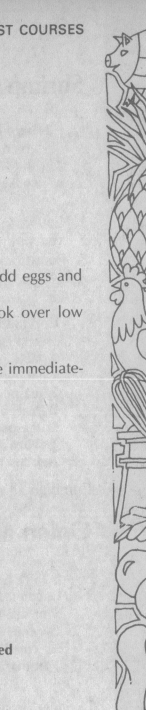

Japanese Egg Roll

1 10 oz can tuna,
   drained and flaked
½ teaspoon salt
3 tablespoons sugar
⅔ cup (166 ml) fish stock
4 tablespoons soy sauce
4 tablespoons sherry

12 eggs, beaten
4 tablespoons olive
   or salad oil
⅓ cup (83 ml) soy sauce
4 tablespoons grated
   radishes

1. Combine tuna, salt, sugar, fish stock, soy sauce and sherry. Add eggs and mix well.
2. Heat oil in a large square frypan. Add egg mixture and cook over low heat, without stirring, until eggs are set.
3. Turn out and roll (as for jelly roll). Cut into six portions.
4. Combine soy sauce and radishes. Pour over egg roll and serve immediately.

Serves 6.

Shrimp Toast

6 slices bread,
   without crust
½ lb (250 g) shrimp, cooked,
   peeled and chopped
¼ lb (125 g) bacon, minced
2 tablespoons minced onion
1 teaspoon salt

1 teaspoon sugar
1 tablespoon cornstarch
3 water chestnuts, minced
   (optional)
2 eggs beaten
bread crumbs

1. Mix together shrimp, bacon, onion, salt, sugar, cornstarch, chestnuts and eggs.
2. Spread mixture on bread and sprinkle bread crumbs on top.
3. Cut into squares and fry on hot oil.
4. Drain and brown the top in the broiler.

Serves 4-6.

Shrimp in Green Pepper Rings

2 large (or 3 medium)
  green peppers
¾ lb (375 g) shelled
  cooked shrimp

½ cup chopped celery
lettuce
chopped parsley
cocktail dressing

1. Cut green peppers into one-inch rings. Place on lettuce.
2. Mix shrimp with celery and fill pepper rings.
3. Pour Cocktail Dressing over the shrimp and garnish with parsley.

Serves 6.

Cocktail Dressing:
½ cup (125 ml) mayonnaise
1 tablespoon tomato sauce
1 tablespoon lemon juice
2 teaspoons horseradish sauce
½ teaspoon paprika
½ teaspoon Worcestershire
  sauce
2 drops Tabasco sauce

Combine all ingredients and chill thoroughly.

Onion and Olive Tart

2 lb (1 kg) onions, chopped
½ cup (125 ml) olive
  or salad oil
1¼ cups plain flour
⅓ cup (83 g) butter
  or margarine

water
10 anchovy fillets
5 tomatoes, sliced
20 black olives, stoned
2 tablespoons chopped parsley

1. Saute onions in oil until golden brown. Remove from heat. Drain, reserving oil.
2. Mix flour and butter or margarine. Add enough water to bind the dough. Roll out on a floured board and line a pie tin.
3. Spread the cooked onions over the pastry. Arrange anchovy fillets, tomatoes and olives on top. Sprinkle with chopped parsley.
4. Pour on remaining oil from the onions and bake in a hot oven 400°F (200°C).

Serves 6-8.

Garlic Shrimp

1 lb (500 g) shelled shrimp
1 tablespoon olive
  or salad oil
2 cloves garlic, chopped

2 teaspoons capers, chopped
1 tablespoon lemon juice
2 teaspoons (10 g) butter
  or margarine

1. Heat the oil in a frypan. Add the shrimp and garlic and cook for 8-10 minutes. Stir constantly.
2. Add the lemon juice and capers and mix well.
3. Stir in the butter and serve.

Serves 4-6.

Mushrooms a la Greque

1 lb (500 g) button mushrooms
½ cup (125 ml) olive oil
2 tablespoons lemon juice
½ lb (250 g) tomatoes,
  peeled

1 bay leaf
2 teaspoons crushed
  coriander seeds
salt and pepper

1. Put olive oil, lemon juice, tomatoes, bay leaf and coriander in a large saucepan and bring to a boil.
2. Add mushrooms and simmer for ten minutes.
3. Season to taste with salt and pepper.

Serves 6-8.

Grapefruit Ring

1 tablespoon gelatin
¼ cup (62.5 ml) cold water
¼ cup (62.5 ml) lemon juice
½ cup sugar

½ teaspoon salt
1 cup boiling water
1½ cups grapefruit pulp
sprigs of mint

1. Soak the gelatin in the water.
2. Mix the lemon juice, sugar, salt and boiling water. Bring to a boil and add gelatin. Remove from heat.
3. When the mixture begins to thicken add the grapefruit.
4. Pour into a wet ring mold and chill until firm.
5. Unmold onto a bed of shredded lettuce and garnish with sprigs of mint.

Serves 4.

Mushroom Ring

1 lb (500 g) fresh mushrooms
1 onion, quartered
4 tablespoons (80 g) butter
or margarine
2 tablespoons flour

1 cup (250 ml) milk
4 eggs, separated
2 tablespoons chopped
parsley
salt and pepper

1. Put mushrooms and onion through a meat grinder or chop very finely.
2. Sauté in two tablespoons of butter or margarine for five minutes.
3. Melt remaining butter in a saucepan, mix in the flour and gradually pour in the milk, stirring constantly. Combine with the mushrooms.
4. Cool and add egg yolks. Mix well.
5. Beat egg whites until stiff and fold into mushroom mixture with the chopped parsley. Add seasonings.
6. Pour into a greased and floured ring mold. Place in a pan of boiling water and bake in a moderate oven 350°F (180°C) for thirty to forty minutes or until set.

Serves 6-8.

Shrimp en Coquille

2 lb (1 kg) shrimp,
    cooked
1 clove garlic
2 tablespoons flour
2 tablespoons (40 g) butter
1 cup cream (250 ml)
½ teaspoon salt

¼ teaspoon pepper
paprika
½ cup (125 ml) tomato sauce
2 tablespoons Worcestershire
    sauce
buttered bread crumbs

1. Rub saucepan well with garlic.
2. Melt butter and add the flour. Mix well.
3. Gradually add the cream, stirring constantly. Cook until thick and smooth.
4. Add the shrimp, salt, pepper, paprika, tomato sauce and Worcestershire sauce. Mix well.
5. Fill shells or ramekins, sprinkle with bread crumbs and cook in a hot oven 400°F (200°C) for about ten minutes.

Serves 8-10.

Crabmeat Cocktail

3 hard-boiled eggs
    (separated)
1 tablespoon (20 g) butter
    or margarine
1 tablespoon prepared
    mustard
½ cup (125 ml) mayonnaise

¼ cup (62.5 ml)
    chili sauce
¼ cup (62.5 ml) vinegar
pinch sugar
¼ cup whipped cream
crabmeat

1. Blend mashed egg yolks with butter or margarine.
2. Add remaining ingredients (except crabmeat) and mix well.
3. Serve over crabmeat and garnish with chopped egg whites.

Serves 8.

Ham and Cheese Crepes

Pancakes:
¾ cup flour
½ teaspoon salt
1 teaspoon baking powder
2 eggs, beaten
1 cup (250 ml) milk
½ teaspoon vanilla

Filling:
¾ lb (375 g) Mozzarella
   cheese
¼ lb (125 g) ham
2 tablespoons butter
2 tablespoons flour
1¼ cups (300 ml) hot milk
salt and pepper
1¼ cups (300 ml) cream
2 egg yolks beaten

1. Sift flour with salt and baking powder.
2. Add beaten eggs, milk and vanilla and mix.
3. Spoon about two tablespoons of mixture onto a small buttered frypan. Tip frypan to spread mixture. When bubbles break, turn pancake and cook on other side. Set aside pancakes until ready to fill.
4. Melt the butter in the top of a double boiler.
5. Stir in flour and cook over simmering water, stirring constantly, until mixture is smooth.
6. Slowly add hot milk and cook, stirring constantly, until mixture is thick. Season to taste with salt and pepper.
7. In a small bowl mix cream and egg yolks. Add about ½ cup of mixture from double boiler and mix well. Pour mixture back into the double boiler.
8. Add ham and cheese and cook, stirring constantly, until mixture is thick and smooth.
9. Spread each pancake with the ham and cheese mixture and roll up. Place in a well-buttered baking dish and bake in a 350°F (180°C) oven for 20-30 minutes.

Serves 4-6.

Cauliflower Mousse

1 large cauliflower
salt
4 eggs
⅝ cup (150 ml) cream
black pepper
nutmeg

1. Cook the cauliflower in boiling salted water until tender. Drain and press through a sieve.
2. Add the eggs and cream to the cauliflower and beat well. Season with pepper and nutmeg.
3. Pour into a well-buttered souffle dish. Place in a pan of boiling water and cook in a 350°F (180°C) oven for 45 to 50 minutes.

(May be served with a Hollandaise or Cheese sauce.)

Serves 6.

Green Beans a la Greque

1 lb (500 g) green beans
½ cup (125 ml) tomato paste
2½ cups (625 ml) water
5 tablespoons olive oil
1 small onion,
   finely chopped
1 small clove garlic,
   crushed
2 tablespoons chopped parsley
salt and pepper

1. Top and tail green beans.
2. Mix tomato paste with water, oil, onion, garlic and parsley.
3. Simmer beans in the tomato paste mixture for 45 minutes, or until sauce has reduced. Serve hot or cold.

Serves 4.

Vegetable and Chicken Soufflé

8 slices bread,
  crust removed
½ onion, grated
½ green pepper, chopped
½ cup chopped celery
1 lb (500 g) cooked
  diced chicken
1 can cream of mushroom
  soup (undiluted)

1½ cups (375 ml) milk
3 eggs, beaten
½ cup (125 ml) mayonnaise
½ cup (75 g) cheddar cheese,
  grated
1 teaspoon salt
¼ teaspoon pepper

1. Place four slices bread in the bottom of a baking dish.
2. Combine onion, pepper and celery with the chicken and spread over the bread. Cover with the remaining four slices of bread.
3. Mix the soup with the milk, eggs, mayonnaise and cheese. Add salt and pepper and mix well. Pour over the mixture in the pan. Bake for 45 minutes in a 375°F (190°C).

(Any leftover meat may be used in place of chicken.)

Serves 4-6.

Scallops Teriyaki

1½ lb (750 g) scallops
½ cup (125 ml) dry sherry
3 tablespoons sugar
3 tablespoons olive
  or salad oil

1½ teaspoon ground ginger
1 clove garlic, crushed
½ cup (125 ml) soy sauce

1. Place scallops in a shallow dish.
2. Mix the sherry with the sugar, oil, ginger, garlic, and soy sauce.
3. Pour over the scallops and marinate for one hour.
4. Drain scallops and place in a buttered baking dish. Bake in a hot oven 450°F (230°C) for 15-20 minutes basting with the sherry mixture and turning occasionally.

Serves 6.

Stuffed Zucchini

8 large zucchini
½ lb (250 g) chopped beef
1 onion, finely chopped
1 tablespoon oil
1 clove garlic, crushed
2 tablespoons chopped
   parsley
1 egg, beaten
1 tablespoon Parmesan
   cheese, grated
4 tablespoons boiled rice
pulp from zucchini
salt and pepper

1. Boil zucchini in water for 3 minutes. Slightly cool. Cut in half lengthwise and scoop out pulp being careful not to break the skin. Reserve pulp.
2. Sauté the beef and the onion in the oil until cooked.
3. In a bowl combine the garlic, parsley, egg, cheese, rice and zucchini pulp. Mix well and season with the salt and pepper. Add to the meat mixture. Blend well.
4. Fill zucchini shells with the mixture and bake in a 375°F (190°C) oven for 20 minutes to ½ hour.

Serves 8.

Spinach Pancakes

Pancakes:
¾ cup flour
½ teaspoon salt
1 teaspoon baking powder
2 eggs, beaten
1 cup milk (250 ml)
½ teaspoon vanilla

Filling:
¾ lb (375 g) cooked
   chopped spinach
½ lb (250 g) cottage cheese
3 eggs, lightly beaten
2 tablespoons Parmesan cheese
½ cup (125 ml) cream

1. Sift flour with salt and baking powder.
2. Add beaten eggs, milk and vanilla and mix.
3. Spoon about two tablespoons of mixture onto small buttered frypan. Tip frypan to spread mixture. When bubbles break, turn pancake and cook on other side. Set aside.
4. Drain spinach well. Combine cottage cheese, eggs, Parmesan cheese and cream with the spinach. Mix well.
5. Spread each pancake with the spinach mixture and roll up. Place in a well-buttered baking dish and chill. Remove from refrigerator ½ hour before baking.
6. Brush each pancake with butter and bake in a 350°F (180°C) oven for 20-30 minutes.

Serves 4-6.

Parma Ham and Melon

½ lb (250 g) Parma ham or Prosciutto
2 large cantaloupes
2 lemons

1. Have Parma ham cut very thinly.
2. Cut cantaloupes into wedges (about nine per melon). Remove seeds and skin.
3. Lay the melon on individual plates and top with slices of ham.
4. Serve with lemon wedges.

Serves 4-6.

Green Bean Soufflé

1 lb (500 g) green beans
2 tablespoons (40 g) butter
  or margarine
1½ tablespoons flour
1¼ cups (300 ml) milk

salt and pepper
3 tablespoons grated
  Parmesan cheese
2 eggs, separated

1. Cook beans in salted boiling water until tender. Drain.
2. Put the butter or margarine in the top of a double boiler and melt over simmering water.
3. Add flour and stir until smooth.
4. Add milk, stirring constantly. Cook over low heat for about ten minutes, stirring constantly. Season to taste with salt and pepper.
5. Remove from heat and stir in cheese and egg yolks.
6. Sauté beans in a little butter in frypan for two minutes. Sieve or purée in an electric blender.
7. Add purée to mixture.
8. Beat egg whites until stiff and fold into bean mixture.
9. Pour into a well-buttered soufflé or casserole dish and cook in a 350°F (180°C) oven for 30-35 minutes.

Serves 4.

Louisiana Shrimp

2 lb (1 kg) shrimp
lettuce
½ cup chopped celery
2 scallions, chopped
1 tablespoon chopped chives
6 tablespoons olive or salad oil
3 tablespoons lemon juice

dash Tabasco sauce
4 tablespoons horseradish sauce
2 tablespoons prepared mustard
1 tablespoon chopped parsley
¼ teaspoon paprika
1 teaspoon salt
½ teaspoon pepper

1. Peel, de-vein and rinse shrimp.
2. Mix together the celery, scallions, chives, oil, lemon juice, Tabasco, horseradish, mustard, parsley, paprika, salt and pepper.
3. Pour over the shrimp and marinate for several hours.
4. Place lettuce on individual plates and spoon on shrimp mixture.

Serves 4-6.

Cream Cheese and Caviar

½ lb (250 g) cream cheese
½ cup (125 g) sour cream
1 tablespoon lemon juice
¼ lb (125 g) red caviar
melba toast

1. Soften the cream cheese.
2. Add sour cream, lemon juice and the red caviar. Reserve one spoonful of the caviar for a garnish on top.
3. Chill and serve with Melba Toast.

Serves 4-6.

Melba Toast
Cut bread into thinnest possible slices. Remove crusts. Put slices in a 250°F (120°C) oven until it becomes crisp and golden brown.

Tuna and Tomatoes on Toast

1 lb (500 g) tomatoes,
   chopped
1 large can tuna
3 hard-boiled eggs,
   chopped
½ green pepper,
   chopped

¼ cup (62.5 ml)
   Worcestershire sauce
½ cup (125 g) butter
   or margarine
½ cup (125 ml) mayonnaise
6 slices bread,
   crusts removed

1. Combine tomatoes, tuna, hard-boiled eggs and green pepper. Add Worcestershire sauce and mix well.
2. Melt 2 tablespoons butter or margarine (40 g) and sauté tuna and tomato mixture until green pepper is tender. Add mayonnaise and mix thoroughly.
3. Melt remainder of butter and sauté the bread on both sides until brown. Sprinkle with a little Worcestershire sauce.
4. Spread mixture on the toast, put slices on a tray and cook in a moderate oven 350°F (180°C) for 8-10 minutes. Cut into triangles and serve hot.

Serves 4-6.

Herbed Shrimp and Avocados

1 lb (500 g) cooked
  peeled shrimp
1 clove garlic,
  crushed
½ cup (125 ml) salad oil
½ cup (125 ml) tarragon
  vinegar

½ teaspoon salt
1 bay leaf
1 tablespoon minced
  parsley
1 tablespoon chopped chives
3 avocados, halved

1. Mix together the garlic, oil, vinegar, salt and bay leaf. Simmer for two minutes.
2. Remove bay leaf and pour over shrimp. Cool and allow to marinate for several hours.
3. Add parsley and chives and toss well.
4. Spoon shrimp mixture over the avocados.

Serves 6.

Coquille St. Jacques

2 lb (1 kg) scallops
2 tablespoons chopped
  parsley
3 carrots, cut up
2 cups (500 ml) white wine
½ teaspoon paprika
1 teaspoon salt
4 tablespoons (80 g) butter
  or margarine

1 tablespoon minced onion
½ lb (250 g) fresh
  mushrooms
4 tablespoons flour
4 tablespoons cream
  or milk
salt and pepper

1. Place the scallops in a saucepan with the parsley, carrots, white wine, paprika and salt. Simmer for ten minutes. Remove the scallops and dice them. Strain the broth.
2. Melt the 4 tablespoons butter or margarine in a saucepan. Add mushrooms and onion and saute for five minutes. Add broth.
3. Combine flour and cream or milk. Add to the mushroom mixture and cook until smooth and thick.
4. Add scallops and season to taste with salt and pepper.
5. Put into eight scallop shells or individual ramekins and put under broiler until lightly browned.

Serves 8

Cottage Cheese Pancakes

Pancakes:
¾ cup flour
½ teaspoon salt
1 teaspoon baking powder
2 tablespoons confectioners' sugar
2 eggs, beaten
⅔ cup (166 ml) milk
⅓ cup (83 ml) water
½ teaspoon vanilla

Filling:
1½ cup (375 g) cottage
  cheese
1 egg yolk
2 teaspoons butter
  or margarine
1 teaspoon vanilla

1. Sift dry ingredients.
2. Add eggs, milk, water and vanilla. Mix but do not beat.
3. Using a small frypan (12 cm or 5 inches), cook very thin pancakes on one side only. Remove from pan when bubbles break and top looks dry. Set aside.
4. Combine cottage cheese, egg yolk, butter or margarine and vanilla. Mix well.
5. Place about 2 tablespoons of cheese mixture on each pancake and roll up. (Fill on cooked side of pancake)
6. Lightly fry filled pancakes in melted butter or oil until golden brown. Turn once.

(May be served with sour cream).

Serves 4.

Pirozhski

Dough:

½ cup (125 g) butter
  or margarine, melted
  and cooled
1 cup (250 g) sour cream

2 eggs
1 teaspoon baking powder
1 teaspoon salt
2 cups flour

1. Combine butter, sour cream and one egg and mix thoroughly. Add baking powder, salt and flour.
2. Roll out thinly and cut into 3 in (8 cm) circles.
3. Place one tablespoon of filling on each circle, fold over and pinch edges together. Brush with remaining egg, beaten.
4. Place onto a well greased tray and bake in a 425°F (220°C) oven for 15 minutes or until brown.

Filling:

1 tablespoon butter
  or margarine
1 medium onion, chopped
1 lb (500 g) ground beef

¼ cup (62.5 ml) beef stock
1½ teaspoons salt
½ teaspoon pepper
2 hard-boiled eggs,
  chopped

1. Heat butter or margarine in a saucepan. Add onion and sauté until golden brown.
2. Add beef and cook until browned. Add stock with salt and pepper and mix thoroughly.
3. Remove from heat and thoroughly stir in chopped eggs.

Serves 6.

Soufflé Puff with Seafood Sauce

  3 **tablespoons (60 g) butter**
     or margarine
  4 **tablespoons flour**
  1 **cup (250 ml) milk**
  2 **teaspoons sugar**
  ¼ **teaspoon salt**
  2 **eggs, separated**
  1 **cup (250 g) sour cream**
     seafood sauce

1. Melt the butter or margarine in a saucepan, add the flour and cook until it bubbles.
2. Add milk, stirring constantly and cook until it thickens. Reduce heat and cook for five minutes. Add sugar and salt.
3. Add small amount of the mixture to the slightly beaten egg yolks and mix well. Add egg yolk mixture to the remaining hot sauce. Beat thoroughly.
4. Beat egg whites until they are very stiff. Fold into the mixture.
5. Line a 8 in by 12 in (20 cm by 30 cm) pan with waxed paper. Butter and flour the waxed paper.
6. Pour mixture into pan and bake in a slow oven 325°F (160°C) for 30-35 minutes.
7. Turn out onto a serving platter and remove waxed paper.
8. Spread with Seafood Sauce and top with sour cream. Cut into sections and serve.

Serve 6.

  Seafood Sauce:
  2 **tablespoons (40 g) butter**
     or margarine
  ½ **cup chopped cooked**
     shrimp
  ½ **cup crabmeat**
  2 **cups white sauce**
  ¼ **cup (62.5 ml) sherry**

Sauté the shrimp and crabmeat in butter or margarine. Add the white sauce and stir in sherry.

Cheese Soufflé

4 tablespoons (80 g) butter **2**	1 teaspoon salt **½**
or margarine	pinch cayenne
4 tablespoons flour **2**	6 egg yolks, beaten **3**
1½ cups (375 ml) milk **3/4**	6 egg whites,
½ lb (250 g) mild cheese, **¼**	stiffly beaten
grated	

1. In the top of a double boiler melt the butter over boiling water. Add the flour and stir until thick and smooth.
2. Add the milk and then the cheese and stir until melted. Remove from heat.
3. Add the egg yolks, salt and cayenne and mix well.
4. Pour onto stiffly beaten egg whites and fold gently until blended.
5. Pour into ungreased casserole or souffle dish.
6. Place in a shallow pan of boiling water and bake in a slow oven 300°F (150°C) for 1¼ hours.

Serves 6. **3**

to fats   7 protein

3/4 bread

3 fats is diet marg

Peach Cocktail

1 cup (250 ml) orange juice	½ cup sugar
2 peaches, pitted	½ cup (125 ml) lemon juice
and peeled	6 ice cubes, crushed
1½ teapoons crushed	
tarragon leaves	

1. Combine all ingredients in an electric blender for twenty seconds on high speed.
2. Serve immediately in chilled glasses.

Serves 6.

Stuffed Green Peppers

6 medium green peppers
1 large can (13 oz) tuna
¼ lb (125 g) black olives
1 small onion,
   finely chopped

3 tablespoons capers
2 tablespoons chopped
   parsley
½ cup (125 ml) olive
   or salad oil

1. Cut off top of peppers and remove the seeds and cores.
2. Combine the tuna with the olives, onion, capers and parsley.
3. Bake in a moderate oven 350°F (180°C) for fifteen minutes.
4. Remove from oven and pour oil over the peppers.
5. Cool and chill for several hours.

Serves 6.

Creole Eggs

2 cans tomatoes (1 lb 12 oz each)
½ onion, chopped
½ green pepper,
   chopped
1 bay leaf
1 cup chopped celery
1 tablespoon chopped
   parsley

salt and pepper
1½ cups fresh
   bread crumbs
1 cup cooked peas
2 cups (250 g) cheddar cheese,
   shredded
8 eggs

1. Mix together tomatoes, onion, pepper, bay leaf, celery and parsley. Cook slowly until celery is tender. Remove bay leaf. Season to taste with salt & pepper.
2. Add bread crumbs and peas and mix well.
3. In individual ramekins pour in a layer of the tomato mixture, then sprinkle on some cheese. Repeat process using up all of the tomato mixture and cheese.
4. Make a depression in each serving with a soup spoon. Break an egg into each depression. Sprinkle with salt.
5. Bake in a moderate oven 350°F (180°C) for twenty minutes or until eggs are cooked.

Serves 8.

Chicken Mousse

3 egg yolks
1½ cups (375 ml) milk
2 tablespoons gelatin
¼ cup cold water
½ cup (125 ml) hot
  chicken stock
1 lb (500 g) minced cooked
  chicken

1 tablespoon lemon juice
salt and pepper
1 tablespoon minced
  parsley
1 cup (250 ml) cream,
  whipped

1. Beat the egg yolks, add the milk and cook in double boiler until it begins to thicken.
2. Soak the gelatin in the cold water, dissolve in the chicken stock and pour into the double boiler.
3. Remove double boiler from heat and add the chicken, lemon juice, salt, pepper and parsley.
4. When cold, fold in the whipped cream. Pour into an oiled mold and chill until firm.
5. Unmold and serve with mayonnaise.

Serves 6.

Melon Cup

1 cup watermelon balls
1 cup cantaloupe balls
1 large can pineapple
  pieces

½ cup (125 ml) syrup
  from canned pineapple
juice of one orange
juice of ½ lemon

1. Chill fruits.
2. Drain pineapple and combine with melon balls.
3. Mix pineapple syrup with orange and lemon juices.
4. Place fruits in individual cups and pour juice over.

Serves 6.

Avocado Cocktail

¼ lb (125 g) bacon
3 avocados, peeled and diced
1 cup chopped celery
1 tablespoon chopped chives

1 tablespoon chopped parsley
½ cup (125 ml) mayonnaise
¼ cup (62.5 ml) chili sauce
juice of one lemon

1. Sauté bacon until crisp. Drain and crumble.
2. Mix the avocado with the celery, chives, parsley, mayonnaise, chili sauce and lemon juice.
3. Serve in cocktail glasses. Garnish with bacon.

Serves 6.

Salmon Mousse

1 lb (½ kg) canned salmon
2 tablespoons gelatin
½ cup cold fish stock
1 cup boiling fish stock
1   cup (250 ml) mayonnaise
1 tablespoon Worcestershire
    sauce

2 teaspoons lemon juice
1 tablespoon finely
    minced onion
salt and pepper
1½ cups (375 ml) cream,
    whipped

1. Soak gelatin in cold fish stock. Add the boiling fish stock and stir until gelatin is dissolved. Cool.
2. When gelatin mixture begins to thicken, add mayonnaise.
3. Beat mixture until frothy. Add salmon which has been finely minced and the Worcestershire sauce, lemon juice, minced onion and salt and pepper to taste.
4. Fold in the whipped cream.
5. Pour into an oiled mold and chill until firm.
6. Serve on shredded lettuce with Cucumber Sauce if desired.

Cucumber Sauce
Peel and finely chop a large cucumber. Add one cup of mayonnaise, 1 teaspoon prepared mustard, one tablespoon lemon juice and one table-spoon chopped chives.

Avocado Ring

1 packet of lime flavored gelatin	1 cup cream, whipped
1 cup hot water	½ cup (125 ml) mayonnaise
3 tablespoons minced parsley	½ teaspoon salt
2 avocados, mashed	1 tablespoon lemon juice
	Lorenzo Dressing

1. Dissolve the gelatin in the hot water. Chill until it begins to thicken.
2. Fold the parsley, avocados, cream, mayonnaise, salt and lemon juice.
3. Pour into an oiled ring mold and chill until firm.
4. Unmold and serve with Lorenzo Dressing.

Lorenzo Dressing:
½ cup (125 ml) olive oil
¼ cup (62.5 ml) vinegar
1 teaspoon salt

pinch of paprika
1 cup chili sauce
1 cup chopped watercress

Mix all ingredients together and chill.

Seafood Salad

1 tablespoon French mustard	½ cup (125 ml) chili sauce
½ teaspoon English mustard	salt and pepper
2 teaspoons Worcestershire sauce	½ green pepper, finely chopped
1 cup (250 ml) mayonnaise	¼ lb (125 g) each shrimp, crabmeat and lobster

1. Mix together the mustards, Worcestershire sauce, mayonnaise and chili sauce. Season to taste with salt and pepper.
2. Mix the sauce with the shrimp, crabmeat and lobster.
3. Serve in individual bowls lined with lettuce. Sprinkle with green pepper.

Serves 4-6.

Baked Noodles

¼ lb (250 g) fine noodles
1 cup cottage cheese
1 cup (250 g) sour cream
1 clove garlic, crushed
1 onion, finely chopped

1 tablespoon Worcestershire
sauce
dash of Tabasco sauce
1 tablespoon chopped
parsley

1. Cook the noodles in salted boiling water until just tender. Drain.
2. Mix the cottage cheese, sour cream, garlic, onion, Worcestershire sauce, Tabasco sauce and parsley.
3. Add to the noodles and mix well.
4. Put in a buttered casserole and bake in a moderate oven 350°F (180°C) for forty-five minutes.

Serves 6-8.

Tomato Soufflé Ring

1 lb (500 g) tomatoes,
peeled and seeded
1 bay leaf
2 cloves
1 teaspoon salt
¼ teaspoon pepper

1 large onion
1 teaspoon sugar
2 tablespoons (40 g) butter
or margarine
4 tablespoon flour
3 eggs, separated

1. Add a little water to the tomatoes and simmer with the seasonings, onion and sugar for ten minutes. Strain through a sieve.
2. Melt the butter, add flour and pour in one cup of the tomato mixture, stirring constantly. Cook until thick. Cool.
3. Add the well-beaten egg yolks to the tomato mixture. Mix well.
4. Beat the egg whites until very stiff and fold into the tomato mixture.
5. Pour into a greased and floured ring mold. Place in a pan of boiling water, cover with a lid and bake in a moderate oven 350°F (180°C) for twenty to thirty minutes.

Serves 6.

Shirred Eggs and Cheese

1 lb (500 g) cheese
1 teaspoon prepared
   mustard
½ teaspoon paprika
1 cup (250 ml) cream

1 teaspoon salt
10 eggs
2 tablespoons chopped
   parsley

1. Cover the bottom of a shallow buttered baking dish with slices of cheese.
2. Mix the mustard, paprika, cream and salt together and pour half of this mixture over the cheese.
3. Break the eggs over this and then pour the remainder of the cream over the eggs.
4. Sprinkle the parsley over the top and bake in a slow oven 300°F (150°C) for twenty minutes or until eggs are set and cheese is melted.

Serves 10.

Mushroom-Egg Mornay

½ lb (250 g) butter
   or margarine
6 tablespoons flour
2 cups (500 ml) milk
½ lb (250 g) cheese, diced
1 lb (500 g) mushrooms,
   sauteed

1 can tomato soup
1 tablespoon Worcestershire
   sauce
2 teaspoons minced
   parsley
salt, pepper, paprika
8 hard-boiled eggs

1. Melt butter in a saucepan. Stir in the flour. Gradually add the milk, stirring constantly. Cook until smooth and thick.
2. Place sauce in the top of a double boiler and add the cheese. Cook until melted.
3. Add mushrooms, soup, Worcestershire sauce, parsley, salt, pepper and paprika to taste.
4. Chop the eggs coarsely and add to the mushroom mixture. Heat thoroughly. Serve on toast.

Serves 8

Tomatoes Stuffed with Avocado

8 large tomatoes
2 avocados
juice of one lemon
1 tablespoon minced onion
1 clove garlic, crushed
salt and pepper

chili powder
2 tablespoons chopped celery
4 tablespoons green
pepper, chopped
2 tablespoons chopped
parsley

1. Slice off the top of the tomatoes and scoop out all the pulp and seeds. Invert on a tray to drain and put in refrigerator until ready to fill.
2. Peel and mash the avocados. Add lemon juice, onion, garlic, salt, pepper and chili powder to taste, celery, green pepper and parsley. Mix well.
3. Fill each tomato with the avocado mixture just before serving.

Serves 6-8.

Fish Soufflé

1 lb (500 g) cooked
white fish
¼ lb (125 g) cooked
peeled shrimp
4 eggs, separated

⅝ cup (150 ml) white
sauce
salt and pepper
parsley to garnish

1. Flake fish and chop shrimp.
2. Mix fish and shrimp with the egg yolks and white sauce. Season to taste with salt and pepper.
3. Beat egg whites stiffly. Gently fold into fish mixture.
4. Pour into a well-buttered souffle or casserole dish.
5. Bake for 35-40 minutes in a 400°F (200°C) oven.

Serves 4-6.

Grapefruit and Crabmeat Cocktail

3 grapefruit
1 can asparagus,
   cut up
1 tablespoon lemon juice
3 tablespoons olive
   or salad oil

½ lb (250 g) crabmeat
1 teaspoon salt
¼ teaspoon pepper
mayonnaise
chopped mint

1. Halve the grapefruit and remove the fruit. Cut the grapefruit into bite size pieces and replace in the skins.
2. Mix the asparagus with the lemon juice, oil, crabmeat, salt and pepper. Spoon onto grapefruit.
3. Top each grapefruit with a little mayonnaise and sprinkle with mint.

Serves 6.

Broiled Scallops

1½ lb (750 g) scallops
¼ cup (62.5 g) olive oil
1 teaspoon salt
¼ teaspoon pepper
2 tablespoons (40 g) butter

2 cloves garlic, crushed
3 tablespoons chopped parsley
1 tablespoon chopped chives
lemons

1. Dip the scallops in olive oil and season with the salt and pepper.
2. Broil for 3-5 minutes on each side. Put in a hot serving dish.
3. Heat the remaining olive oil with the butter, garlic, parsley and chives. Pour over the scallops.
4. Serve with lemon wedges.

Serves 6.

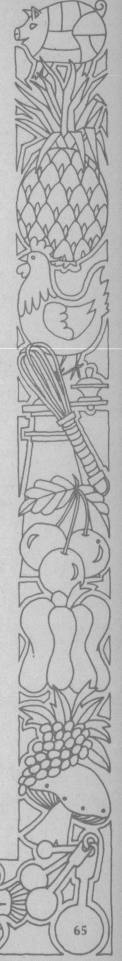

Chicken Almond Mousse

1½ tablespoons gelatin
3 cups (750 ml) chicken
  stock
1 teaspoon salt
½ teaspoon pepper
2 teaspoons finely
  chopped onion
¼ teaspoon paprika
3 egg yolks

½ cup (80 g) finely
  chopped almonds
3 cups chopped cooked
  chicken
1 cup (250 ml) cream,
  whipped
lettuce
lemon wedges

1. Soak the gelatin in ½ cup cold chicken stock.
2. Combine remaining stock with the salt, pepper, onion and paprika in the top of a double boiler.
3. Stir a little of the hot stock mixture into the egg yolks and mix well. Return to the stock mixture.
4. Cook the egg yolk and stock mixture over hot water until smooth and thick, stirring constantly.
5. Blend in gelatin and remove from heat. Cool.
6. When partially thickened, fold in almonds, chicken and whipped cream.
7. Pour into oiled mold and chill until firm.
8. Unmold onto a bed of lettuce leaves and serve with lemon wedges.

Serves 6.

Artichokes Polonaise

3 cans artichoke
  hearts (14 oz each)
½ cup (125 g) butter
  or margarine
1 tablespoon olive oil
½ cup cracker crumbs
2 hard-boiled eggs,
  finely chopped

2 tablespoons chopped
  parsley
1 small clove garlic,
  crushed
¼ cup (62.5 ml) white wine
2 tablespoons tomato sauce
salt and pepper

1. Heat artichoke hearts in their own liquid.
2. Melt butter in a frypan. Add oil, biscuit crumbs, eggs, parsley, garlic, white wine and tomato sauce. Season to taste with salt and pepper.
3. Drain artichoke hearts and place in serving dish. Pour the sauce over the artichokes.

Serves 8.

Eggs Florentine

2 cups chopped cooked spinach	1½ cups (225 g) grated processed cheese
6 eggs	2 tablespoons chopped parsley
1 can cream of celery soup	

1. Line the bottom of a shallow buttered baking dish with the spinach.
2. Make six depressions in the spinach and break an egg into each one.
3. Heat the soup (undiluted) and add one cup of cheese. Stir until cheese is melted.
4. Pour the cheese and soup mixture around the eggs. Sprinkle with the remaining ½ cup of cheese and parsley.
5. Bake in a moderate oven 350°F (180°C) for 30 minutes or until eggs are cooked.

Serves 6.

Shrimp Fritters

1 cup (250 ml) water	1 cup (125 g) grated cheese
4 tablespoons (80 g) butter	¾ lb (375 g) cooked peeled shrimp, cut into small pieces
1 cup flour	
4 eggs	

1. Bring water to a boil with the butter.
2. Add flour all at once, stirring well until mixture leaves the side of the saucepan.
3. Remove from heat and add well-beaten eggs. Stir until smooth and thick.
4. Stir in shrimp and cheese.
5. Drop by small spoonfuls into shallow hot fat. Brown on both sides.

Serves 6.

Artichokes Vinaigrette

artichokes
(one per person)

Vinaigrette Sauce:
1 tablespoon lemon juice
2 tablespoons vinegar
¼ teaspoon dry mustard
salt and pepper

8 tablespoons olive
or salad oil
2 teaspoons chopped
parsley
2 teaspoons finely
chopped onion
2 teaspoon chopped
chives

1. Remove the outer leaves of the artichokes. Trim the stem. Cook in a large saucepan of boiling salted water for 30-40 minutes. (Artichokes are cooked when a leaf pulls off easily.) Drain well and cool.
2. Mix together all the ingredients of the Vinaigrette Sauce. Beat well and chill.
3. Artichokes are eaten by tearing off a leaf at a time, dipping the meaty end in the Vinaigrette Sauce and eating the tender base of each leaf. Then remove the fuzzy centre and eat the artichoke heart.

(Artichokes may also be eaten hot with the leaves dipped in hot melted butter.)

Asparagus Polonaise

2 bunches fresh asparagus
1 tablespoon (20 g) butter

Sauce:
½ cup (125 g) butter
  or margarine
2 cups fresh bread crumbs

3 hard-boiled eggs,
  chopped
2 tablespoons chopped
  chives

1. Wash the asparagus well and trim the hard ends.
2. Cook asparagus in a shallow saucepan. Lay them flat and cover with boiling water. Add butter to the boiling water. Cook until just tender about 10-15 minutes. Drain and place on serving dish.
3. Melt the butter or margarine in a saucepan. Add bread crumbs and sauté until lightly browned.
4. Add eggs and chives and mix well. Pour over the asparagus and serve immediately.

Serves 6.

Fish Cocktail

½ lb (250 g) cooked white
  fish, flaked
½ teaspoon salt
2 tablespoons lemon juice
2 tablespoons capers

½ cup tomato sauce
1 tablespoon prepared
  horseradish sauce
lettuce leaves and
  chopped parsley

1. Mix the salt, lemon juice, capers, tomato sauce and horseradish sauce together.
2. Gently mix in the fish.
3. Place in individual dishes lined with lettuce leaves and garnish with chopped parsley.

Serves 4.

Pears with Cream Cheese

4 ripe pears
⅛ lb (62.5 g) blue cheese
1 tablespoons (20 g) butter
    or margarine
¼ cup (62.5 ml) milk

¼ lb (125 g) cream cheese
salt and pepper
2 teaspoons chopped parsley
lettuce leaves
paprika

1. Peel the pears, cut in half and remove the cores.
2. Cream the blue cheese with the butter or margarine.
3. Fill the pears with the blue cheese mixture.
4. Blend the milk and cream cheese. Season to taste with salt and pepper. Add parsley and mix well.
5. Place the pears on the lettuce leaves, pour the cream cheese mixture over the top and garnish with paprika.

Serves 4.

Cheese and Corn Soufflé

2 tablespoons (40 g) butter
    or margarine
4 tablespoons flour
1¼ cups (300 ml) hot milk
salt and pepper

¼ lb (125 g) cheddar cheese,
    grated
4 tablespoons creamed corn
3 large eggs, separated

1. Melt butter in the top of a double boiler. Stir in flour and cook over simmering water for three minutes.
2. Remove from the heat and slowly add the milk, stirring constantly. Return to the heat and cook for a further five minutes or until thick and smooth.
3. Add salt and pepper to taste. Blend in cheese and corn.
4. Remove from heat and add beaten egg yolks. Blend well.
5. Beat the egg whites until very stiff and fold into the cheese and corn mixture.
6. Pour into a well-buttered soufflé or casserole dish, place dish in pan of boiling water, and bake in a 325°F (160°C) oven for 40-45 minutes.

Serves 4.

Shrimp Creole

1 green pepper
1 onion
1 stalk celery
4 tomatoes
2 cups cooked peeled
  shrimp

2 tablespoons (40 g) butter
  or margarine
salt and pepper
½ cup chicken stock
2-3 cups cooked boiled rice

1. Slice the pepper into strips.
2. Peel the onion and chop finely. Cut celery into slices. Peel and chop tomatoes.
3. Sauté the shrimp in the butter or margarine for two minutes. Add salt and pepper to taste.
4. Add vegetables and saute for ten minutes.
5. Add stock and cook for another ten minutes.
6. Serve on top of boiled rice.

Serves 4.

Eggs Mornay

8 hard-boiled eggs
2 cups (500 ml) white sauce
2 tablespoons grated
  Parmesan cheese

2 tablespoons chopped
  parsley

1. Peel and slice the eggs. Lay the eggs in a well-buttered baking dish.
2. Blend white sauce and Parmesan cheese.
3. Pour over the eggs.
4. Garnish with parsley.
5. Brown under a broiler for a few minutes.

Serves 4-6.

Spanish Flan

Pastry:
1 cup cake flour
1 tablespoon (20 g) butter
  or margarine
¼ teaspoon salt
pinch pepper
½ cup (125 ml) mayonnaise

Filling:
1 tablespoon olive
  or salad oil

2 large onions, chopped
4 zucchini, sliced
2 cloves garlic, crushed
4 large tomatoes,
  peeled and chopped
salt and pepper
1 tablespoon chopped
  parsley
1 tablespoon chopped
  chives

1. Rub the butter or margarine into the flour, salt and pepper.
2. Add the mayonnaise and mix to a soft dough.
3. Roll out and line a flan tin.
4. Bake in a 400°F (200°C) oven for 10 to 15 minutes or until golden brown. Set aside.
5. Sauté onions, zucchini and garlic in the oil for five minutes. Add tomatoes and sauté for 5 more minutes. Season to taste with salt and pepper.
6. Fill flan with vegetables, garnish with parsley and chives and heat for ten minutes in oven.

Serves 6.

Avocado and Shrimp

3 large avocados
3 tablespoons olive
   or salad oil
3 tablespoons vinegar
¼ teaspoon salt
¼ teaspoon pepper
½ teaspoon dry mustard

1 small clove garlic,
   crushed
½ lb (250 g) cooked shrimp,
   peeled
lettuce leaves
lemons

1. Halve the avocados and remove the seed.
2. Combine the oil, vinegar, salt, pepper, mustard and garlic. Beat well.
3. Toss the shrimp in the dressing and spoon onto the avocados.
4. Place on lettuce leaves and serve with lemon wedges.

Serves 6.

Broiled Grapefruit

3 large grapefruit
2 tablespoons (40 g) butter
   or margarine
3 tablespoons honey
1 teaspoon mixed spice

1. Halve the grapefruit and loosen segments from the skin. Remove as many pips as possible.
2. Return segments to grapefruit shells.
3. In a small saucepan, heat butter or margarine with the honey and the mixed spice until butter is melted.
4. Pour over the grapefruit and broil for about five minutes.

Serves 6.

Shrimp Provencale

1 lb (500 g) shrimp, cooked and peeled	3 tomatoes, peeled and chopped
2 tablespoons (40 g) butter or margarine	¼ lb (125 g) mushrooms, sliced salt and pepper
3 tablespoons olive oil	1 tablespoon chopped parsley
1 medium onion, sliced	lemon juice
1 clove garlic, crushed	

1. Heat the butter and oil together. Sauté the onion and garlic for 2-3 minutes.
2. Add the tomatoes and the mushrooms and sauté for another five minutes.
3. Add the shrimp and cook until the shrimp are heated through.
4. Season to taste with salt and pepper.
5. Serve sprinkled with parsley and lemon juice.

Serves 4-6.

Stuffed Cucumber

3 medium cucumbers	1 tablespoon chopped chives
½ cup cooked chicken, chopped	½ cup mayonnaise
½ cup cooked shrimp, chopped	2 tablespoons lemon juice
1 stalk celery, finely chopped	2 tablespoons tomato sauce
2 tablespoons chopped parsley	1 tablespoon chili sauce
	salt and pepper

1. Peel cucumbers (if desired) and cut in half lengthwise. Scoop out seeds and set aside.
2. Mix together chicken, shrimp, celery, parsley and chives.
3. Blend together mayonnaise, lemon juice, tomato sauce and chili sauce. Season to taste with salt and pepper.
4. Mix the dressing with the chicken and shrimp.
5. Spoon mixture into cucumbers.

Serves 6.

Spinach Ring with Mushrooms

2 teaspoons grated onion	1 t
1 tablespoon (20 g) butter or margarine	1½ fats / ¾ fat
2 cups cooked spinach, chopped	1 cup
½ cup dry bread crumbs	¼
2 egg yolks	1
1 teaspoon salt	
½ teaspoon paprika	
2 tablespoons (40 g) butter or margarine	¾ fat
2 tablespoons flour	1 ⅓ bread
¼ teaspoon salt	
1¼ cups (300 ml) hot milk	½ + 2 T
¼ lb (125 g) fresh mushrooms	⅛ lb
1 tablespoon (20 g) butter or margarine	¾

1. Sauté the onion in 1 tablespoon butter until golden brown.
2. Add spinach, bread crumbs, beaten egg yolks and salt and paprika. Mix well.
3. Pour into a well-buttered ring mold set in a pan of boiling water.
4. Bake for 30 minutes in a 350°F (180°C) oven.
5. Melt 2 tablespoons butter or margarine in a saucepan. Remove from heat and mix in flour and salt. Cook until it bubbles. Slowly add milk, stirring constantly. Cook until mixture thickens.
6. In another saucepan, melt the 1 tablespoon butter or margarine and cook the mushrooms for three minutes.
7. Add to cream sauce and mix well.
8. When spinach ring is cooked, unmold and fill center with mushroom mixture.

Serves 4-6.

Tuna Fish Mold

3 tablespoons (60 g)
   butter or margarine, melted
6 egg yolks
1½ cups (375 ml) milk
1 tablespoon sugar
¼ cup (62.5 ml) vinegar

1 teaspoon dry mustard
salt and pepper
2 tablespoons gelatin
4 tablespoons cold water
large can tuna fish (13 oz)

1. Combine the butter or margarine, egg yolks, milk, sugar, vinegar, mustard and salt and pepper to taste.
2. Cook in the top of a double boiler until thick, stirring constantly.
3. Dissolve gelatin in cold water and then add to the egg yolk mixture. Mix well.
4. Add tuna fish and blend thoroughly.
5. Pour into an oiled mold and chill until firm.
6. Unmold onto a bed of lettuce.

Serves 6.

Herring Salad

2 cans pickled herring
2 medium green apples,
   peeled, cored and chopped
½ cup cooked beets
   drained and chopped
1 lb (500 g) potatoes,
   cooked peeled and diced
2 tablespoons chopped parsley

2 teaspoons chopped chives
2 tablespoons olive
   or salad oil
3 tablespoons vinegar
salt and pepper
2 hard-boiled eggs, chopped
lettuce leaves

1. Cut the herring into small pieces.
2. Mix the herring with the apples, beets, potatoes, parsley and chives.
3. In a small jar, put the oil and vinegar, salt and pepper and shake well.
4. Put the lettuce leaves on individual dishes, spoon on the salad and sprinkle with the dressing. Garnish with chopped eggs.

Serves 6.

Chicken Vol-Au-Vent

8 vol-au-vent
pastries
3 tablespoons (60 g) butter
or margarine
6 tablespoons flour
½ cup (125 ml) dry white wine
2½ cups (125 ml) chicken stock
salt and pepper

1 lb (500 g) cooked
chicken, diced
¼ lb (125 g) button
mushrooms
1 egg yolk
2 tablespoons cream
2 tablespoons chopped parsley

1. Melt the butter or margarine in a small saucepan. Add the flour and, stirring constantly, cook for 2 minutes.
2. Slowly add the wine. Mix well.
3. Gradually add the chicken stock, stirring constantly.
4. Season to taste with salt and pepper. Cook for ten minutes.
5. Add chicken and mushrooms and reheat.
6. Remove from heat. Mix egg yolk and cream and add to the chicken mixture. Blend well.
7. Fill the vol-au-vents and heat thoroughly in a 350°F (180°C) oven, garnish with chopped parsley.

Serves 8.

Leeks a la Greque

6 medium leeks
1 teaspoon dried tarragon
1 tablespoon lemon juice
1 clove garlic,
    crushed
2 tablespoons chopped
    parsley
2 tomatoes, peeled
    and seeded

pinch thyme
salt and pepper
1 bay leaf
¼ cup (62.5 ml) olive
    or salad oil
1 cup (250 ml) water

1. Cut off tops of leeks. Wash thoroughly.
2. Combine all ingredients in a heavy-bottomed saucepan.
3. Cover and bring to a boil. Reduce heat and simmer for about ten to fifteen minutes.
4. Remove from heat and cool. Serve chilled.

Serves 4-6.

Crab Mousse with Caviar

1¼ cups (300 ml) mayonnaise
1¼ cups (300 ml) cream
1 teaspoon thyme
salt and cayenne
1 lb (500 g) crabmeat

1 tablespoon gelatin
2 tablespoons cold water
1 small jar caviar
lettuce leaves

1. Mix together mayonnaise, cream, thyme, salt and cayenne to taste.
2. Flake crabmeat and add to the mayonnaise mixture. Mix well.
3. Mix the gelatin with the cold water. Put over hot water until the gelatin is dissolved.
4. Blend the gelatin with the crabmeat and mayonnaise mixture.
5. Pour into an oiled mold and chill until firm.
6. Unmold onto a bed of lettuce leaves.
7. Top with caviar.

Serves 4-6.

Welsh Rarebit

2 tablespoons (40 g) butter or margarine
3 cups (375 g) grated Cheddar cheese
½ teaspoon dry mustard
½ teaspoon salt

pinch of cayenne pepper
1½ teaspoons Worcestershire sauce
½ cup (125 ml) beer
2 egg yolks
hot toast

1. Mix together the cheese and the butter or margarine in the top of a double boiler. Place over simmering water and stir until cheese melts.
2. Add mustard, salt, cayenne pepper, Worcestershire sauce and beer. Cook over boiling water for five minutes.
3. Remove from heat and stir in slightly beaten egg yolks.
4. Spread over slices of hot toast.

Serves 4.

Cheese Ravioli   *Too much flour*

3 eggs
2½ teaspoons salt
2 cups flour, sifted   *32 T / 16 = 5 bread*
3 cups cottage cheese   *use 1½*

3 tablespoons cream
1 teaspoon salt
pinch of pepper

1. Beat eggs lightly. Add salt and flour. Knead well, cover and let stand for about 30 minutes. Roll out very thinly and let stand for one hour to dry. Cut into 3 inch (8 cm) wide strips.
2. Combine cheese, cream, salt and pepper. Make into small balls. Place on one side of strip about one inch (2½ cm) apart. Cover with other side and press the edges together. Cut into individual squares, pressing the edges together and let dry on a floured cloth for two hours.
3. Cook a few at a time in boiling salted water for about fifteen minutes. Drain and saute in butter. (May be served plain or with a sauce of your choice.)

½ ree   a protein   1 milk
5 breads   1½ protein

Serves 6-8.

78

Index